LEO THE SNOW LEOPARD

The true story of an amazing rescue

Told by JULIANA HATKOFF, ISABELLA HATKOFF, and CRAIG HATKOFF

SCHOLASTIC PRESS / NEW YORK

We dedicate Leo's story to the next generation of global citizens and problem solvers. We hope it serves as an example of the role and importance of cooperation in finding solutions to the planet's seemingly intractable problems, as well as those problems that do not yet exist but surely will.

Photo credits: Front jacket and case: Kamal-ud-Din. Back jacket and case: Karl Schuler / IUCN. Pages 4, 8-9, 11 © Karl Schuler. Pages 10-17, 22-23 © Doug Kuzmiak. Page 12 © Kamal-ud-Din. Pages 18-21 © WCS. Pages 24-32 © Julie Larson Maher/WCS. Map on page 34: Courtesy of Jim McMahon.

All rights reserved. Published by Scholastic Press, an imprint of Scholastic Inc., *Publishers since 1920.* SCHOLASTIC, SCHOLASTIC PRESS, and associated logos are trademarks and/or registered trademarks of Scholastic Inc.

Library of Congress Cataloging-in-Publication Data

Hatkoff, Craig.
Leo the snow leopard / by Craig Hatkoff. —1st ed.
p. cm.

1. Snow leopard—New York (State)—New York—Juvenile literature. 2. Wildlife rescue—Pakistan—Juvenile literature. 3. New York Zoological Park—Juvenile literature. I. Title.
QL737.C23H379 2010
599.75'55—dc22
2009041043

ISBN 978-0-545-22927-2
10 9 8 7 6 5 4 3 2 1   10 11 12 13 14

Printed in Singapore 46
First edition, October 2010

The text type was set in Garamond.
Book design by Elizabeth B. Parisi

We would like to thank everyone at the Wildlife Conservation Society, the Bronx Zoo, World Wildlife Fund, and International Union for Conservation of Nature for all of their help rescuing and caring for Leo the snow leopard. We would also like to thank: Allison Stern, Katharina Otto-Bernstein, Natalie Cash, Mary Dixon, Humaira Khan, Doug Kuzmiak, Mayoor Khan, Julie Larson Maher, Pat Thomas, Kamal-ud-Din, Sajid Ali, Sophie Bass, Peter Zahler, Jennifer Rees, Rachel Mandel, Laura Morgan, and Kristin Earhart, whose invaluable contributions made this book possible. We would also like to thank Leo, who has brought the plight of the snow leopard to the attention of the world.

For more information about our growing collection of true animal stories, please visit www.turtlepondpublications.com, www.owenandmzee.com, www.knut.net, www.miza.com and www.scholastic.com/miza, www.winterstail.com and www.scholastic.com/winterstail, and www.leothesnowleopard.com.

Dear Reader,

   We have been privileged to go on an amazing literary journey and have traveled far since our first book, the now-famous Owen & Mzee. From North America (Winter the dolphin) to Africa (Owen, Mzee, and a mountain gorilla named Miza) to Europe (Knut the polar bear), we now journey to Asia to the Himalayan Mountains in Pakistan to tell the story of Leo the snow leopard.

   There are two zoos that hold a magical place in our hearts: the Central Park Zoo, located just a few blocks from our current home on the island of Manhattan, and the world-famous Bronx Zoo. When we first met with our friends from the Wildlife Conservation Society (WCS) who oversee these national treasures, it was clear that there were many wonderful stories about the thousands of animals who live at these zoos and the dedicated people who take care of them. One story stood out immediately. It was the story of Leo. Orphaned at a young age (it's unclear what became of his mother), little Leo was found, rescued, and sheltered by a local goat herder. Leo quickly grew too big, however, and was turned over to Pakistani authorities. Caring for a snow leopard in captivity is no small feat, but every problem calls for a solution. In an effort that required enormous collaboration between the United States and Pakistan, Leo began an epic journey to the Bronx Zoo.

   A three-person scientific team from WCS embarked on a dangerous journey to bring Leo to New York. When Dr. Pat Thomas and Dr. Peter Zahler told us the story of Leo's daring rescue firsthand (and showed us their magnificent photographs), it felt almost like a real-life Indiana Jones movie. The team traveled up the narrow roads of the Karakoram mountain range north of the Himalayas and home to the second highest peak in the world, K-2. With massive rockslides possible at any moment, the scientists had to first get to Leo, then travel with him by truck to Islamabad, where an official "handing over" ceremony and press conference was held before his long trip to the Bronx Zoo.

   Only a few thousand snow leopards remain on our planet, and scientific study and breeding programs will help us better understand what is necessary to ensure survival of the species. Successfully breeding Leo would add valuable genetic diversity that will help preserve this endangered species. Leo's story sets an example of international cooperation and fills us with great hope. We are pleased to induct Leo the Snow Leopard into the Turtle Pond Collection.

With love and hope,

Craig Hatkoff   Juliana Hatkoff   Isabella Hatkoff

This is the true story of a baby snow leopard named Leo, an orphan who was too young to be on his own, in the wild, without a family or a home. It is also the story of the many people who bravely came to Leo's rescue.

It is not easy to be a snow leopard who needs his mother and doesn't have one. Likewise, it is not easy to be a human who needs to rescue and care for a wild animal. But Leo and the people who saved him went to extraordinary measures to help one another. This is their amazing story.

One bright, crisp day in the snowy Karakoram mountain range in northern Pakistan, an incredible thing happened. A goat herder discovered a baby snow leopard. Under normal circumstances, a person would not want to be anywhere near a snow leopard cub, because its mother—fiercely protective of her young—is sure to be somewhere close by. But these were not normal circumstances: This cub appeared to be on its own. After a long period of careful watching and waiting, the man was certain the snow leopard was in trouble. The cub's mewing went unanswered. He was lost and probably very hungry. He was all alone.

The goat herder could not turn his back on the little cub and walk away. So he did the only thing he could think of to do. His heart racing, he gently picked up the cub, stroked his soft fur, and took him to a place where he could feed him and keep the little orphan safe: his own home.

Surrounded by towering mountains with rugged cliffs and snowy peaks, Naltar Valley is both beautiful and dangerous.

Without a mother, or someone to care for him, Leo is helpless.

No one knows for certain how the tiny cub came to be orphaned, or how long he had been on his own. A snow leopard stays with its mother for the first two years of its life. This time is crucial for cubs to learn how to be snow leopards: how to take care of themselves, how to hunt for food by stalking prey, and how to avoid wolves, brown bears, and humans. When the kind goat herder found the orphan, the cub was much too young to survive on his own.

It must have been quite a shock for the goat herder's children to find a snow leopard nestled in their father's arms when he returned home that day. They knew all about snow leopards, of course; but they never expected one to appear in their home! The family fed the cub goat's milk and spoke encouraging words. The cub adapted surprisingly well, playing with the children and sleeping on their laps. He seemed to like the attention!

A curious Leo takes in new smells, sounds, and sights.

Soon the cub grew too large and frisky, and needed to be moved into a grain shed in the family's yard. About this time, he seemed to become listless and tired. The goat herder worried that he wouldn't be able to care for the cub much longer, so he contacted the World Wildlife Fund offices in Pakistan. The World Wildlife Fund (WWF) is an organization that works to protect nature, keeping endangered animals and pristine places safe. The organization sent a group to meet the cub in Naltar and take him to their offices in the city of Gilgit. The goat herder's family was sad to see the cub go, but they knew they had done the right thing.

At the WWF offices in Gilgit, veterinarians examined the cub. They determined that he was dehydrated and needed more liquid in his body, and they estimated that he was only about seven weeks old. Wildlife staff member Kamal-ud-Din was to take care of him. Kamal had training and experience with wild snow leopards, but even so, would he be able to nurse the cub back to health?

Everyone helps Leo feel safe.

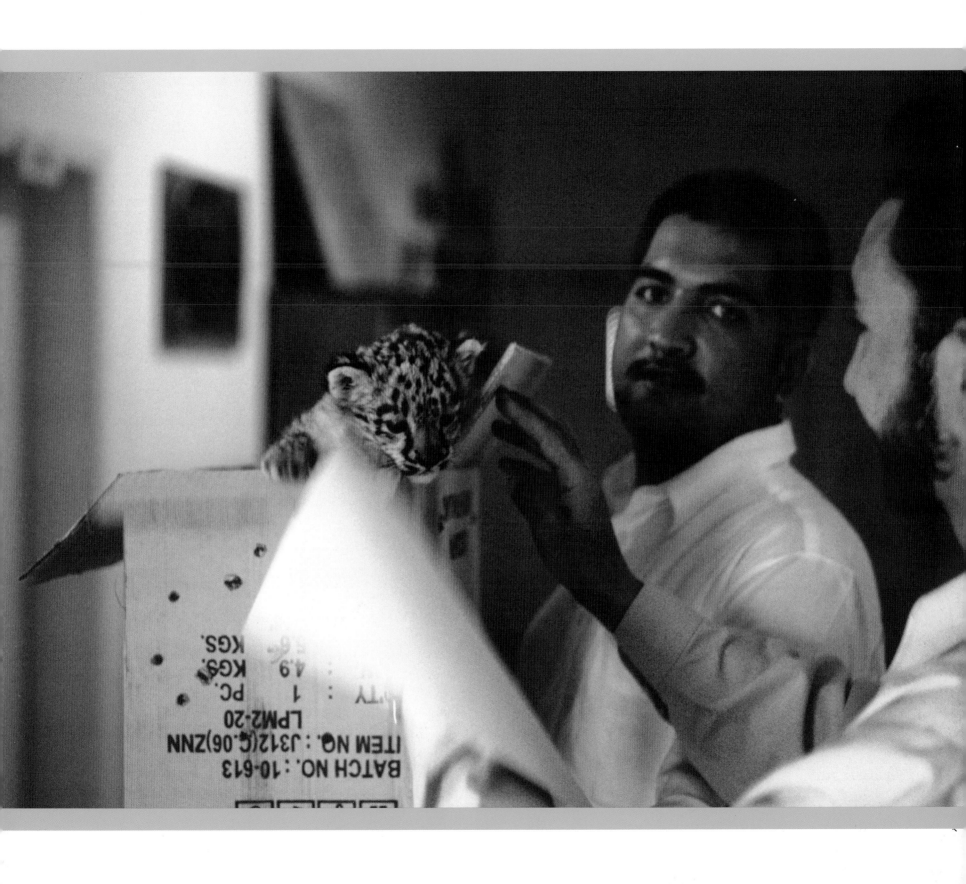

BATCH NO. : 10-613
ITEM NO. : J312(G.06)ZNN
LPM2-20
Q'TY : 1 PC.
4.9 KGS.
KGS.

Kamal named the cub Leo, after the small mewing sound he made. It was a call that the cub would have used to communicate with his mother. Now Kamal was acting as the cub's mother, and Leo would call out to him. Kamal learned to interpret the cub's sounds and anticipate his needs as best as a human could. With the help of the Wildlife Division of the Government of Pakistan, Kamal moved Leo to a special home within Khunjerab National Park, which is known for its wild snow leopard population.

Pakistani officials wanted to do what was in the best interest of the snow leopard species. They contacted the United States Embassy, hoping they could help find a place for Leo to stay until Pakistan could build a new wildlife center. And because snow leopards are on the International Union for Conservation of Nature (IUCN) Red List of endangered species, Leo's welfare was now a matter of global importance.

Soon, the United States Department of State was in touch with the Wildlife Conservation Society (WCS), an organization that saves wildlife and wild places. WCS is also in charge of the famous Wildlife Conservation Society's Bronx Zoo, a leader in keeping and breeding snow leopards. With over seventy cubs born there and a staff of qualified scientists, everyone agreed that the Bronx Zoo would be a superb home for Leo.

Leo quickly recovers, thriving under Kamal's care.

Obtaining the paperwork and approvals for moving an endangered animal from one side of the world to the other is a tremendous task. There are international laws that protect endangered species, and these laws control when and how an animal can be moved. The United States Department of State worked closely with Pakistan to ensure that Leo's journey would be a safe one.

WCS arranged for a team of three scientists to fly to Pakistan to accompany Leo back to the United States: Bronx Zoo Curator of Mammals Dr. Pat Thomas, WCS wildlife veterinarian Dr. Bonnie Raphael, and WCS Assistant Director for the Asia Program Dr. Peter Zahler.

The WCS team flew into Islamabad, Pakistan's capital. The group was anxious to meet Leo, but first they had a treacherous seventeen-hour drive ahead of them. The narrow road was carved out of the side of the steep mountains, while rocky cliffs plunged toward the crashing white rapids of the Indus River below. But the drop was not the only concern. Avalanches could rain down from above, and that's just what happened. A landslide brought their jeep to a dead stop. With the road blocked, the crew had to leave the jeep and climb over the rubble.

From left, Dr. Pat Thomas, Dr. Bonnie Raphael, and (right) Dr. Peter Zahler.

Kamal reaches his hand past the bars to lovingly rustle Leo's fur.

The team was exhausted when they arrived in Naltar Valley, but Leo was an inspiring sight. At thirteen months, he was playful, energetic, and spry. He lived in a sturdy shed with an outdoor enclosure, so he could get plenty of fresh air. Even at play, Leo was impressive. He played pouncing games with Kamal and seemed to love the attention! The WCS team needed to determine if Leo was healthy enough to travel. Fortunately, he received a clean bill of health. Kamal would miss Leo, but he knew everyone was doing what was best for the snow leopard.

When it was time to leave, Leo climbed into a wooden travel crate with little hesitation, showing great faith in people. Leo was ready for the road. Unfortunately, the road was not ready for him. The landslide the team had encountered on the way had not yet been cleared, so the group loaded the snow leopard into a jeep, drove to the landslide, and carried Leo in the cage over the shifting rubble. Then they placed their precious cargo in a different jeep, and the group made their way to Gilgit, where Leo would have his first formal ceremony to celebrate his journey.

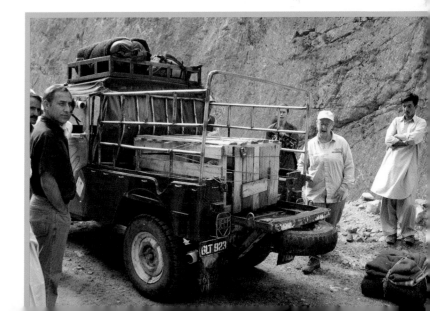

In his special crate, Leo is a first-class traveler.

Because everyone worried that Leo would overheat under the summer sun, they stayed in a hotel with air-conditioning. Leo acted like a seasoned traveler, eating and resting well. During their stay, they learned that a flash flood had torn a bridge from its banks, blocking their way to Islamabad. They would have to wait for a temporary bridge to be built. As long as Leo could keep an eye on one of his traveling companions, he seemed calm.

When they finally reached Islamabad, there was more fanfare. Leo and his team stayed in a first-class hotel, where Leo was fed chicken and lamb off an elegant serving platter! Leo had become a national celebrity. The Pakistani people were proud of the snow leopard, and there was a big ceremony to celebrate his journey to the United States. The ceremony was a chance to recognize the extraordinary level of teamwork that it had taken to get Leo this far. Many people and organizations had put in a great effort to make arrangements, always putting Leo's well-being first.

Dr. Pat Thomas speaking at Leo's send-off ceremony.

Leo sniffs out his new home, and seems to like it.

Leo's first plane ride took him from Islamabad to London, England, and then on to New York City in the United States. Once he arrived in the Bronx, he was quarantined for thirty days at the zoo's Wildlife Health Center, which is a safeguard for all new residents of the Bronx Zoo. It keeps them from spreading potential illnesses to the other animals, and it allows the veterinarians and zoo staff to take necessary tests and learn about the incoming animals as well.

Leo remained an easygoing cat. He continued to connect with people, making affectionate chuffling noises (similar to loud, rhythmic purrs) when he saw his traveling companions Dr. Thomas and Dr. Raphael. His affinity for people had made the transition to his new life easier, but it had become clear that Leo thought of himself as a person, not a wild cat.

Soon, it was time for Leo's grand debut at the Bronx Zoo.

Leo gets ready to settle down for a nap.

The first lady of Pakistan, Sehba Musharraf, attends a special ceremony for Leo.

With large outcroppings of rock and lush layers of greenery, Leo's new home reflected the rugged terrain of his natural mountain territory. Following his instincts, Leo gracefully leaped to the top tier of the habitat, where he could survey his surroundings. The shy, elusive nature of the snow leopard was on full display as he rested on the sun-dappled boulders. He seemed relaxed and content, even with the excited crowd gathered to welcome him. Likewise, he did not arouse much curiosity from his new neighbors in the Himalayan Highlands exhibit, the red pandas and white-naped cranes.

Leo's arrival at the zoo was a triumph for everyone who had helped along the way. The people of Pakistan had agreed to send Leo to the Bronx Zoo because it was beneficial to Leo as well as snow leopards as a species. Everyone hoped that Leo would, in time, become a father to new cubs. Captive breeding programs help ensure the survival and diversity of endangered species. Zoos give scientists the opportunity to learn more about animals, especially reclusive species like the snow leopard, so they can help them thrive in the wild.

A snow leopard can use its long tail to help steer, like the rudder on a boat.

While it is helpful for zoo animals to be accustomed to people, the goal is for them to be as true to their nature as possible. Leo needed to learn about being a snow leopard from another snow leopard, so the zookeepers introduced him to Shelby. Shelby was born at the Bronx Zoo, and she was Leo's age. Zoo staff also hoped that one day she would be his mate.

Leo's keepers were not sure how Leo would react to Shelby—or how she would react to him—so they allowed them to slowly spend more time together. Each cat was appropriately wary of the other, and it was clear Leo was uncertain of what to do. He lingered around his den, keeping a close eye on his keepers. The two snow leopards eventually approached each other, but Leo did not seem to pick up cues from Shelby's posture or expressions. It took him time, and some warning swipes from Shelby, to understand that when Shelby was crouched down with her ears back, she was unhappy. And when she greeted him with a warm chuffle, she was being friendly.

At first, Leo does not know how to interact with another snow leopard.

Thanks to Shelby, Leo knows how to properly groom himself.

Shelby was a good teacher, and now Leo behaves more like a true snow leopard. He knows how to groom himself and read Shelby's signals. He is also very playful, pouncing on Shelby or batting at her legs as she trots away.

Of course, Leo still shows great interest in the people around him. He spies on workers from above and follows his keepers around his enclosure, jumping expertly from one perch to another along the way. He delights in a good game of hide-and-seek, ducking behind a log or bush and "stalking" his keepers. Despite having grown into a sleek and regal big cat, he remains lively and friendly. He vies for attention from his keepers and Shelby alike, and calls happily when he receives it.

While Leo has come a long way, his past will always be part of him. He would not have survived on his own without people's help, and we hope his rescue and his story may benefit the snow leopards that remain in the wild.

Snow leopards prefer high perches. Here, Leo is content.

Snow leopards by nature are survivors. They withstand almost impossible conditions—frigid snow, harsh winds, unsteady ground. Though Leo had lost his mother, his survival instincts enabled him to persevere. But he needed help to find a home. Eventually traveling halfway around the world, Leo quickly became a striking symbol of a snow leopard's beauty, grace, and strength. He also became a symbol of international teamwork and goodwill among individuals and organizations, and between nations. Leo is now an ambassador for snow leopards—and other endangered species—everywhere. Leo, along with those who helped make his journey possible, are an excellent example of how problems can be solved through cooperation. Leo and his story provides hope that, if we all work together, nothing is impossible.

Snow Leopards

Scientists know less about snow leopards than they do about any other big cat. This is due, in part, to the leopard's mountain habitat, which is so high and so steep and with weather conditions so extreme that few people travel to that elevation. It is also due to the very nature of the snow leopard: incredibly secretive. The pattern of the snow leopard's fur, a pale cream or gray with dark rosettes, serves as camouflage on the rocky terrain. A snow leopard is also a smart cat, knowing to avoid contact with humans. From the first years of life with its mother, a snow leopard learns that humans are one of its few enemies. Interestingly, many people in these regions regard snow leopards as sacred animals; these elusive big cats appear on various coats of arms and in old country lore.

Snow leopards live in the upper elevations of the mountain ranges of Central Asia, ranging from Russia, Mongolia, and China through Pakistan and Afghanistan to India and Nepal. A single snow leopard's territory depends on how much prey is available: The less food in a region, the more land the snow leopard covers trying to get enough to eat. A snow leopard might range anywhere from five to more than two hundred square miles. Most active at dawn and dusk, the snow leopard leaves a trail of scent markings and claw rakings to communicate with other cats whose territories overlap with his. These solitary cats normally meet only during breeding season.

As one may well imagine, living in the high mountains can be treacherous. The freezing temperatures and rocky cliffs are far from warm or easy to navigate, but snow leopards have what it takes to survive in this harsh environment. Their lush coat insulates them from the cold in the frigid winters. A tail that is almost as long as the cat's body provides balance when the cat leaps from cliff to cliff; it also serves as a warm, fluffy scarf while the snow leopard sleeps. Thick fur covers their paws, providing traction to keep them from slipping in the deep snow. While snow leopards are born with all of these tools, they still need to learn how to survive. It is the mother's job to teach them these life lessons.

Wildlife Conservation Society

The Wildlife Conservation Society (WCS) is dedicated to saving wildlife and wild places. Founded in 1895 as the New York Zoological Society, the organization had an inspiring set of goals: 1) to improve wildlife conservation; 2) to promote the study of zoology; and 3) to create a first-class zoo. These objectives inspire WCS's efforts to this day.

Now WCS is in charge of four zoos and an aquarium, all located in New York City. In 1903, the Bronx Zoo, Leo's home, was the first zoo in the Western Hemisphere to exhibit snow leopards. The first cubs were born there in 1966, and more than seventy have arrived since. In a collaborative effort, the Bronx Zoo has sent snow leopards to more than thirty zoos in the United States as well as in Australia and eight countries throughout Europe, Asia, and North America.

In the wild, WCS is as committed as ever to conserving both habitats and animals. They work in over 60 countries and 75 landscapes, and on hundreds of species, using state-of-the-art methods and partnering with concerned individuals and governments locally, nationally, and internationally. Even before the goat herder rescued Leo, WCS was involved in conservation efforts in this biologically rich and geographically remote mountainous region. Since 1997, WCS has assisted local communities in northern Pakistan to manage forests and wildlife in a sustainable manner.

Zoos and Captive Breeding

The first public zoo opened in 1779 in Vienna, Austria. Originally an imperial animal collection reserved for the royal family and guests, the Schönbrunn Zoo was on the palace grounds. With its opening to common people, it offered visitors a first glimpse at animals that seemed beyond the visitors' wildest imaginations.

The goal of the world's premier zoos changed from entertainment to research and conservation. Now many zoos work together, or collaborate, in the care of endangered species. By studying and caring for these animals in captivity, the researchers and scientists learn how to better protect animals in the wild. It requires careful observation and dedication. The zoo professionals share their findings with one another, allowing for better care throughout the network of zoos that are committed to preserving species in captivity and the wild.

One way to ensure the survival of threatened species is through captive breeding, that is, zoo animals having babies. Leo's arrival at the Bronx Zoo held promise for the captive breeding program. It is important to have fresh bloodlines to ensure the health of future generations of animals. It is rare to introduce a truly wild animal into a captive breeding program, so everyone hopes Leo will become a father and help maintain the integrity of snow leopard genes in captivity.

Leo has been a true ambassador for snow leopards. The more people who appreciate the beauty and power of this species and understand its struggle, the better its chances of survival. Leo's transfer to the Bronx Zoo generated a lot of attention for snow leopards, including, in part, a 2008 international conference in Beijing that produced action points necessary for saving the species. Also, it has inspired cooperation between the Bronx Zoo and Pakistani wildlife experts in designing a wildlife rehabilitation center in Pakistan in hopes that Leo might one day be able to return to his homeland.

Endangered Species and International Laws

The International Union for Conservation of Nature (IUCN) created the Red List of Threatened Species to help conserve animal and plant species. Species on the list are at risk of becoming extinct, and, with their numbers dropping to between 3,500 and 7,000 in the wild, snow leopards are red-listed.

Snow leopards face three major threats. The first is poachers, people who illegally kill snow leopards for their fur, which is worth a lot of money. The second threat is their dwindling food supply. Snow leopards primarily feed on wild sheep and wild goats, and the numbers of many of these species are falling, also due in part to a decreased food supply. Local herders are moving into the territory of the wild sheep and goats, so the herders' animals are grazing on the grass that the wild sheep and goats would normally eat. This competition for food causes the wild sheep and goat numbers to drop, which forces hungry snow leopards to hunt animals from the herders' flocks. The third threat are the herders who sometimes will shoot snow leopards to protect their own animals or in retaliation for livestock that has been killed by the cats.

The IUCN Red List lets us know which species are in danger. There are also international laws protecting endangered and threatened species. Transporting Leo from the mountains of Pakistan to the Bronx Zoo required a lot of effort from a great number of people. The Convention on International Trade in Endangered Species of Wild Fauna and Flora (CITES) is an international agreement among governments that works to make sure that any international trade in threatened animals protects the species at risk. The government of Pakistan needed to issue an export permit for Leo to leave its country, and the United States had to issue an import permit for Leo to enter. While it seems like a lot of paperwork, these laws help ensure that our planet's plants and animals will survive.